The F.I.X.

(Focused & Intentional eXecution)

7 Steps to Climbing the Corporate Ladder Without Sacrificing Your Health or Neglecting Your Family

By Dana L. Cox

Printed in the United States of America

First Printing, 2023

ISBN: 979-8-9876523-0-5

Edited & Formatted by Show Your Success

Published by Dana L. Cox

Dedication

To my Pumpkins, You are the JOY of my life. Your enthusiasm for learning and exploring new ideas fills me with hope and inspiration. I have written this book for you—so that one day when you look back, you can take pride in knowing that I wrote something special just for you.

I would like to take this time to express my utmost gratitude and appreciation for the unconditional love and support from my children, Aleslíana, Dominic, Auston-James, Trevor, Christopher, and Jonathan. You have been a source of strength in times of difficulty and JOY in times of celebration, providing me with a sense of comfort and happiness that only family can bring. I am proud of each one of you for your accomplishments, and continue to learn valuable life lessons from you every day. Thank you all for being an amazing part of my life. I love you!

To my hubby, I am forever grateful for the encouragement and love you have given me. From inspiring me to follow my dreams no matter how crazy they may seem to being there through the ups and downs—you have been my ROCK, my Ride or Die. Your unwavering belief in me has given me the confidence to take on anything I put my mind to, including this project, and I can't thank you enough for your support. You are truly a blessing in my life.

With all my love and admiration.

Table of Contents

Foreword

There is a multitude of insight offered to leaders on how to be successful. From the "Eight Hacks of Highly Productive People," or "Six Daily Habits of Highly Successful People." Rarely do we hear about or even talk about in our inner circles or the tremendous sacrifices that are made in the pursuit of success.

Being a leader is one of the greatest gifts that you can offer mankind. However, it's a tough and rocky journey to embark upon, filled with high highs and low lows. While it is rewarding, people rarely talk about the sacrifices that it takes to become successful.

The recent resignation of Jacinda Ardern, the Prime Minister of New Zealand, citing burnout, highlights the multitude of challenges encountered at work, even if you're at the top level of government. It's never ending.

In this AMAZING book, Dana is sharing insight on how to climb the corporate ladder without sacrificing your health or neglecting your family. Take this insight from someone who has not only talks the talk, but she's walked the walk.

I can't wait for you to get this insight and APPLY IT so you can become better for yourself FIRST and your family. You deserve better than just having a dream job. You deserve a DREAM LIFE too. It's waiting for you.

Christy Rutherford
Women's Leadership Expert
Executive Coach to Bada$$ Women
ChristyRutherford.com

Foreword

Kathleen Jaramillo Kweskin LMT RYT RMT
CEO & Founder of Grow Wellness

As an alternative medicine practitioner and the CEO of Grow Wellness, I am constantly in pursuit of inspiration and personal balance so that I can best serve the world around me. Dana's book nurtured that pursuit, and as I sat down to simply begin the first chapter, I found myself in the same chair until I finished the entire book. With the turn of every page, I was empowered and enlightened as I read about the wisdom she has accumulated over the years so eloquently represented to benefit others. Dana has continuously scaled as a businesswoman, all the while embodying her values by extending the ladder behind her to help others. She is a genuine force of nature that can be trusted to uplift and inspire those around her.

Dana and I met professionally at a pivotal point in her journey; she was first a client and a student. I have been her yoga and meditation instructor, Reiki practitioner, herbalist, and massage therapist for six years. Throughout our time together, a friendship blossomed as we supported each other in our goals and business endeavors. I have had a front-row seat to watch

Dana's dedication to personal development, wellness, leadership, and business strategy. I have continued to be in awe and feel honored to have gotten to be a part of her journey. She has found her authentic recipe for success, and she put in the work and the passion for finding that recipe. I remember so many moments as she explored yoga, meditation, and energy healing where a light would click behind her eyes as she discovered what worked for her success on all levels. Outside of her practice at Grow Wellness, she continued to put in the work of studying with mentors, researching on her own, and attending group leadership events. With every experience in her career and personal life, Dana took the time to learn from them. Let's also not forget that she has traveled the world and brought a wide scope of insight to her journey.

Every year, Dana's career has scaled. The size of the team that she leads grows continuously, and her experience in the field is extensive. Her endeavors and goals have also grown, adding more and more countries to her travel journeys and taking on business owner roles of her own. This incredible blossoming did not happen magically. Dana has put in the work, the research, the passion, and dedication to create this effortless flow of success and wellness.

This book is invaluable; she shares the wisdom that took her decades to uncover with readers. Anyone who picks it up will be better for it and empowered on their journey of self-development and the pursuit of authentic purpose.

Acknowledgments

I would like to begin this book acknowledgment page by thanking God for blessing me with the opportunity to write and share my thoughts. Without His guidance, I would not be here today.

To my village: my mom, Theresa, my late father, Terry, my late grandparents (Susie, Earlean, Ruth, and Roosevelt), who are ALWAYS with me, and my godmothers, Cynthia and Henrietta. Thank you ALL for your unwavering support throughout my life, even the course corrections. Your love, care, and guidance have been instrumental in helping me make the right decisions in life and enabled me to build a strong foundation for the future.

To my tribe, JAG, my China Doll Sisters, The Original Eagle Crew, especially my girl "Frack," Janeczka Lee, my coaches Christy Rutherford and Raquel Naranjo, and the entire Vision Finder International family. You have supported me and pushed me to realize the magnitude of the value I possess. Thank you for being the ultimate HYPE women and encouraging me to take the limits off.

To Kathleen Kweskin and my Grow Wellness family, thank you for creating an oasis of peace and tranquility that is a refuge and place of peace where I have been able to reconnect with myself on my continuous journey of self-discovery, growth, and healing.

Taurea Vision Avant and my Book Profits Club team, you are DOPE beyond measure and have been an amazing source of support throughout the entire process. Your enthusiasm and dedication made this project possible, for which I owe you a great debt of gratitude.

Finally, I would like to thank all of the preorder supporters. Thank you for your support. I am forever grateful!

Stephanie Banks, Stephen Chapple, Leandra Morris, A Well Made Woman, Emily Simon, Robyn Shavers, Oneaka Hendricks, Christine Miller, Mara Cristina Tache, Aleeta A. Gardner, Janeczka Lee, Berke Baydu, Tiffany Kobashigawa, Deonte Key, Brad Stillman, Stephanie Welsh, Orla Regan, Lorraine Durkin, Bshani International, Mark Workman, Sarah Peck, Discover Your Bliss Network LLC, Amanda Daniel, Ryan Beaudry, Geisha L. Lawrence, Pierre-Michel Durieux, Lee Barker, Linda Becker, Orphelia Rivers, Amy Marie Grinna, Alexis Hall, Denis Korolev, Fitness Boss LLC, Kamesha Lewis, Dominic Brown-Cox, Spring Burgess, Perfect Pitches by Precious LLC, Tony Conte, Erica McNeal, R&E Holdings Group LLC, Simon McNiel, Jo A Gold, Kathy Roy, Sally Rose, Ebony Walker Jones, Doraina Walker-Williams, Jonathan Brown-Cox, Christine Santori, Sheldon Jackson, The DEI Coach, Natasha Green, Toni Gillespie, Valeria Key,

SECTION 1

THE ASSESSMENT

Introduction

I have a dear friend, maybe you know her. Don't tell her I am telling you her story. She is a high-achieving, high-performing, successful woman leader in corporate America. She pours everything she has into her career and is known as the "fixer" that can handle any project or endeavor that has gone off course. She spends her free time reading leadership and self-help books and getting that extra degree or certification. Why? Because she is sure that all of these will gain her more promotions and recognition and cement her value in the minds of her employer. Remind you of someone?

What many don't see is this same brilliant, fabulously put-together woman is drowning. No amount of back-to-back yoga classes, ashwagandha in her tea, 2-hour massages, or happy hours spent commiserating with friends can bring her the peace of mind she desperately needs. Sound familiar, ladies? All the luxurious self-care options are failing her; she is tired and at her wit's end. Why?

The secret to excellence in leadership lies within you right now. It begins with trusting that small voice inside of you that says when it's time to stay or go—and busting a move with precision. That little voice is saying you are doing this all wrong. Times have changed. Have you? Oh yes, it's time to bring the real you out!

How often do we, as women, look to others for validation in knowledge, leadership ability, strength, and empowerment? Yet, we often overlook those unique, intrinsic qualities we already possess. What we already have does not mean anything to us until someone else sees it and recognizes it. I am not implying that we discard or ignore the value of education or hard work, yet my plea to you is that we all must first and foremost see the beauty, talent, skill, and abilities in ourselves before others will recognize it. Then, focus and reflect on the value we each bring to the table. Only then, when our internal is congruent with the external, does the real magic happen! It is when you become comfortable in your power that others will become comfortable with your power. Let me say that again! When you become comfortable in your power, others will become comfortable with your power.

I know, easier said than done, right?

Sometimes, I doubted my ability to lead. I would look at other leaders in awe and think they brought more to the table, so I made myself smaller and stayed in the background. Sometimes, I felt all success was linear and a step-by-step process. If I only worked harder, then my leadership would recognize my skills! Outside validation was what mattered.

I didn't allow myself to dare and go after what I wanted for fear of what others would think and speak.

I used to tell my dreams and goals to the wrong people and let them talk me out of it! I look back and want to smack myself! Why tell your BIG dreams to small minds and those who aren't trying to be better themselves?

Now, I encourage all of you to have the faith to know that what you want is possible. We are all in the process of Becoming!

My spirit told me to tell you TODAY what others won't. To tell you what I wished I had heard more of as I grew up in a world that did not understand that women leaders come in all shapes, sizes, colors, and backgrounds and that women could indeed be transformative leaders. We are all different as women, which is part of natural diversity. Bring ALL of you to the table.

Writing is a conversation, not a monologue. Knowing there are people like you who are genuinely interested in what I have to share is an indescribable feeling. It is my sincere hope that your life is touched in some way as a result of reading this book, and I thank you for taking this journey with me.

So if you are an ambitious woman looking to take your career development and personal growth to the next level to prepare you to scale the corporate ladder and achieve ALL you deserve, let this book be the starting point for you. If you need support implementing the steps outlined in this book, meet me at **bonus.thefixbook.com**.

CHAPTER 1

Discovering Your Blindspots

"The most common blind spot is believing
others have them, but you don't."
~ Author Unknown

A s women, we need to be aware of the potential blindspots we may face in the workplace as we look to climb the corporate ladder. Blindspots can involve barriers such as access to resources, networks, and mentors, gender stereotypes and bias, or lack of opportunities for career growth. We need to be mindful of how our decisions and actions are perceived by others, including peers and leaders alike. Additionally, it is important for us to recognize that there is no one-size-fits-all solution to achieving success—each of us must find our unique path forward based on our specific experiences. By being aware of these potential blindspots, we can make informed choices about how best to move forward confidently in our professional journeys.

Who are you?

When you walk into a room, how do you show up? Are you showing up as your authentic self or as a representative of yourself? Being authentic means being true to oneself and allowing one's true thoughts, feelings, beliefs, and values to be expressed openly in any situation. A representative of oneself only exhibits a dimension of the authentic self—a fragmented or incomplete version of you, which involves presenting oneself in a way that is assumed socially acceptable and appropriate in the given context. So, are you adjusting how you behave or present based on what you ASSUME is most suitable for the environment you are in? Are your assumptions based on your experience (which may or may not be true) or facts about the situation, environment, or people you interact with? Do people see and experience the REAL you or your representative? Inquiring minds want to know.

You need to understand who you are at your core, which provides you with the background and landscape for your true authentic self to emerge and manifest. It is important to know your "self" when addressing blind spots to make informed fact-based decisions vs. emotionally charged assumption-based responses. Knowing your 'self" can help you identify or experience your strengths and weaknesses, empower you to better understand how others view your behaviors and decisions or experience you, allowing you to address these blindspots which impede your ability to climb the corporate ladder. Overall, self-awareness is a crucial skill if you are looking to improve and succeed on your personal growth journey.

What are you hiding?

I think a lot of us mask what's really going on. You have your Coco Chanel pins, Christian Louboutin red bottoms, the perfect power jacket, or that 100% Virgin Remy Indian hair down your back, or you have some funky frames, your eyebrows are arched just so, your nails are popping....but you are drowning on the inside. Because you've made the decision to mask all the discomfort, all the dissatisfaction, you're masking all the frustration as if no one can see it. When the reality is, Sis, you ain't fooling nobody. PERIODT! Half the time your slip is hanging out, and the truth is you don't have anyone in the community telling you what you need to hear; they are just filling your head with what you want to hear.

I remember when I was working at the bank, and there was a leader who was in such a hurry, just moving and moving, trying to do a hundred and one things, but when she came out of the bathroom, her entire dress was tucked into her pantyhose. I ran up behind her and informed her, first, don't turn around because I was providing her coverage, and second, take a moment to adjust her clothing. She was shocked, embarrassed, and physically shaking. She didn't realize her state because it was behind her—it was a blindspot. Often it's the things that we don't see, can't see, or refuse to acknowledge that reveal our true state to those around us. It can even be how you say things. It is not what you say but how you say it; the tone does matter. Are you coming across as abrasive? Do people prefer NOT to work with you on assignments? You are not aware of this because you believe you are approachable. You are secretly angry and frustrated with your life or circumstances, but the reality is you are melting people's faces off.

Assess Joy Deferred

Let's dig into this deeper. How many of you are from families with humbled beginnings (aka Poor)? I, myself, was born and raised in the inner city of Milwaukee, Hillside Housing Project, to be exact. Did you move into a career or line of study that was not your first passion or love? Have you ever questioned whether you are living your authentic life or somebody else's? Did you study what you wanted to study, what brought you joy and excitement, or what your parents said you ought to study? Or did you pick your major based on the cute boy you were dating or wanted to date? Oh wait, maybe that was just me...LOL! For the record, he was FINE! But let me get back on track.

Because a lot of us are the ones for our family, and we have to find a way, by hook or crook, to get that degree. You become really good at something, whether it's cheerleading, volleyball, basketball, pick a sport, any sport, fill in the blank, because that becomes the catalyst to how the doors to college got opened for you. And, you enter a field of study that you felt compelled to or encouraged to by your family, and you are miserable because it wasn't what you really wanted to study. We weren't really living the life that we wanted and are now here we are, 34, 45, 58, 63, finally starting to tap into that.

Why have I been this angry woman at my job? What's this? Why is it that when my colleague takes a particular action, I am irritated? Frustrate me? Hell, downright trigger me? And when you take the time to assess the situation and follow that line all the way back, it stems from the fact that you had to do something other than what you loved. So every time you encounter somebody that forces you, in a sense, to do something that wasn't really what you wanted to do, it triggers you, and then you act a darn fool, and it impedes your growth and your further development. You are intrinsically doing things that don't bring you joy.

So, ask yourself the question, what are the things that bring me joy? Now, think about those things, assess if you could do ANYTHING, what it would be? Be clear and intentional about choosing things that bring you joy.

Are you addicted to outside input?

We talked about this earlier about self-belief. We tend to look to others for validation of our worth, to validate our knowledge, abilities, strengths, or empowerment, and we overlook the unique and intrinsic qualities we already possess. Why is this?

It's funny (ironic, not haha) because it's like what you have doesn't mean anything to you until someone else sees it and recognizes it. Always looking for external validation. You can have a million dollars in your hand, but to you, it's just a pile of paper. It's not until someone else says, "Oh, Dana, that's a million dollars," that you see its value - $1 Million. Why is that? Why can't you see how bright, intelligent, beautiful, and resourceful you are? Why do you need someone else to recognize those things in you to give it credence or credibility? You can qualify it yourself. You don't need someone else to qualify you.

It's like we feel like we have to go through some type of certification program and get stamped "APPROVED" or "Certified by Inspector 17." What is that all about?

Chapter 1 - Summary - Discovering Your Blind Spots:
- Unleash the REAL You
- Take Off Your Mask(s) to Unlock Your True Joy
- Divorce Yourself from External Validation and Gain Self-Awareness

---

Chapter 1 - Reflection: Discovering Your Blindspots

Identify three blindspots you didn't realize or have forgotten about that are getting in the way of you realizing your goals.

_____

_____

_____

_____

_____

_____

_____

_____

What skills or attributes might be helpful to remediate the blindspots you have identified?

_____

_____

_____

_____

_____

_____

_____

_____

_____

What actions are you committed to taking? Who will you ask to hold you accountable?

_____

_____

_____

_____

_____

_____

_____

_____

_____

Identify "Dimming" Behavior

"You dimming your lights is not doing anyone any favors, especially not yourself - it's your time to shine."
~ Author Unknown

I know what you are thinking. I'm successful and I'm doing all the things; I can't possibly be dimming my light. But there are two types of light-dimming behavior (LDB). There's someone else dimming your light or you dimming your own by your actions or lack thereof. Understanding the self-imposed behaviors that dim your light and have the potential to negatively impact your climb up the corporate ladder is of significant importance. LDBs are like ninjas; they are sneaky, subtle, and stealthy. They may have even served you well before, but what got you here, what keeps you here, certainly won't get you where you want to be. So let's look at some examples of LDBs.

Are you a Name-Dropper?

Name-dropping is a necessary evil that must be well-managed. There is a thin line that should not be crossed. You may start out utilizing someone else's name to establish a relationship, but that can subtly morph into an LBD. Are you a name-dropper? Or do you use the names of others to qualify what you say or to give the statement more credibility than if it came from you? When you do this, you are giving that person's title or experience a higher value than acknowledging the value you bring based on your experience and expertise.

Name-dropping can be a tempting habit to fall into as you look to climb the corporate ladder; however, it can have a detrimental impact on your credibility if used too much. When you are using name-dropping in excess, not only can it be seen as an attempt to gain favoritism or impress others with connections, but it also establishes you more as a messenger than as a leader...Is that really what you are going for?

Additionally, when you rely too heavily on name-dropping, people can view you as disingenuous and inauthentic, basically giving you the side eye, and it can make it difficult for you to establish meaningful relationships. So basically, what I'm saying is there is a time and place for everything, so be selective and thoughtful when name-dropping, as you want to ensure the names and information add value to the conversations rather than detract from them.

Finding your own voice is essential when climbing the corporate ladder, as speaking up and expressing your opinions can help establish your credibility and personal brand and provide you with a platform to advocate for yourself. I'm reminded of some sage advice my Gram used to tell me, "you have two ears and one mouth," so it's equally important that you practice active listening to the ideas and perspectives of others without judgment. This helps to drive more meaningful conversations, and doing so will demonstrate empathic respect for the viewpoints of others.

Are you Playing Small?

I'm sure I'm not the only one that has entered a conference room where there were no assigned seats, yet I chose to take a seat on the wall versus at the table. Or what about when others come to a meeting late, do you stop focusing on the meeting to help them find a place to sit, or move your things to make room for them? Or my personal favorite when being either the only woman or one of a few, are you the one that volunteers to take the minutes or put in the lunch order, as if you are the meeting secretary? Playing small is a common LDB among women in the workplace and tends to show up through behaviors like underselling their own skills, not celebrating their accomplishments, downplaying their successes, not speaking up in meetings out of fear of being perceived as aggressive, deferring to others when you are the expert in the room.

Ultimately playing small is a self-limiting behavior that can prevent you from capitalizing on opportunities or advancing in your career. These types of behaviors should be actively avoided to reach your full potential. Take the limits off! You are a BADAss, and you've earned the right to not only be in the room but to sit at the table and NOT take the darn meeting minutes or put in the lunch order. Stop playing small! Make *This Little Light of Mine* your theme song. Don't allow anyone to blow your light out or to hide it under a bushel...Not Even YOU!

This Little Light of Mine (Author Unknown)

This little light of mine, I'm going to let it shine
All around the neighborhood (corporation),
I'm going to let it shine
Hide it under a bushel? NO! I'm going to let it shine.
Let it shine, All the time, Let it shine

The Story of You

One thing common in leadership workshops or trainings is the ability to deliver the 60-second elevator pitch in a personable, clear, succinct, and memorable manner. Here's the scenario; you walk onto the elevator at work, and there is a senior-level executive with whom you don't have a relationship, but you have 60 seconds or less to share the Story of YOU. Who are you? What do you do? And why is it important to them? Can you do it?

Not being able to speak about yourself compellingly is an LDB that can have a significant impact on your career prospects. Being able to articulate and present your accomplishments, experiences, and aspirations is essential for your success. Unfortunately, many of us struggle to do so because we feel uncomfortable promoting ourselves or our work. However, a lack of self-promotion can lead to missed opportunities for advancement or recognition. You must recognize your own abilities, learn how to confidently discuss your achievements and successes, and advocate for yourself to be successful.

The ability to self-promote requires the courage to speak confidently about yourself and what you have accomplished, as well as help you advocate when it comes to job opportunities or salary negotiations. Without the ability to self-promote, you risk being overlooked or undervalued, and believe it or not, you may even find it difficult to get noticed in the hiring process.

> ***Chapter 2 - Summary - Identify Diminishing Behaviors:***
> - Be Seen as a Leader by Strategically Managing Name-Dropping
> - Act Like a Queen to Be Treated Like a Queen
> - Get Clear on Your Story and Tell It!

Chapter 2 - Reflection: Identify "Dimming" Behavior

Are you demonstrating any LDBs? If so, list the LDBs you are demonstrating that are getting in the way of you realizing your goals.

_____

_____

_____

_____

_____

_____

_____

_____

What is the WHY behind these LDBs?

_____

_____

_____

_____

_____

_____

_____

_____

What actions are you committed to taking? Who will you ask to hold you accountable?

_____

_____

_____

_____

_____

_____

_____

_____

_____

SECTION 2

THE PLAN

CHAPTER 3

Establish a blueprint

"There are dreamers and there are planners;
the planners make their dreams come true."
~ Edwin Louis Cole

Making it to the top of the corporate ladder isn't easy for everyone—it requires a lot of hard work and dedication. It's definitely not easy when there are few role models or when the role models are non-existent. What I've found in my own personal journey is it was not enough to have the aspiration, but it was necessary to have a blueprint for success if I wanted to make sure my career and life stayed balanced. Climbing higher in one's profession can often come at the expense of other areas; there is an intrinsic opportunity cost. Having a blueprint to outline your true North will enable you to reach your goals without sacrificing what's important to you.

Start with your values

It is important to determine your values before you are presented with a situation where they are tested. Your personal values serve as your foundation and ensure you have a clear understanding of what you believe in and are an invaluable source of strength when the bottom drops out and the ISH hits the fan. The higher you ascend the corporate ladder, the more ambiguous, gray, and amorphous the space. Your value system has to be firmly established to dictate what your personal true North is—whether or not one is being provided. Visit **bonus. thefixbook.com** for the Core Value Clarity Journal.

My personal values—service, integrity, humility, and empathy—are non-negotiable. They are the core of my being and determine how I live and move, as they serve as a dynamic litmus test to keep me aligned with my true north. I believe in putting the needs of others above my own and serving those that I lead, coach, and mentor with an attitude of service and respect. I strive to build a culture of trust and collaboration that is based on mutual respect and open communication. My goal is to ensure that my leadership style leaves a legacy and fosters an environment where my team members feel valued and empowered to make decisions, work towards goals, and strive for excellence whether I'm there or not.

Analyze Your Gaps

When I'm interviewing people, I am not only looking at their current skills, but I'm also looking at their potential. Individuals that are confident in their current capabilities can articulate the value they can add now and in the future. It is essential to evaluate your skills and capabilities when planning to climb the corporate ladder to determine what strengths you can leverage and what areas need improvement for success—a.k.a, Gap Analysis. Now it is important that when completing this evaluation, you are not wearing "rose-colored" glasses. While I know I'm all of that and a bag of chips, and you may be too, we must be honest with ourselves if we really want to achieve success; what we don't want to do is introduce new blind spots.

When conducting your gap analysis, don't just look at hard skills but also soft skills such as communication, leadership abilities, and problem-solving, as these are often just as crucial for your success. Additionally, having a realistic understanding of your skill level/proficiency can help determine which positions would be the best fit for you as you navigate your career journey.

The first step I take when engaging a client is I conduct a skills assessment (a.k.a. Gap analysis) of their hard and soft skills, potentially leveraging their job description for this exercise. Other tools we can leverage are past performance reviews or an aptitude test. However, one of the best tools is 360 feedback. Obtaining feedback from people you like and like you is easy, but the best feedback you receive is from those that you have challenging relationships with. Soliciting feedback from people that you may find difficult to work with or may perceive you difficult to work with helps uncover blind spots. Visit **bonus.thefixbook.com** for the Skills Evaluation Process.

Be clear on your destination

It's always important to know where you are going; otherwise, how will you know when you have arrived? You don't take a trip without having a destination in mind, so why would you leave your career up to fate? That makes absolutely NO sense whatsoever.

Getting clear on your career goal is important to achieve success in your professional life. Taking the time to reflect on what makes you passionate and what would make you happy professionally can help you determine which direction to pursue. Once you have identified a few potential career paths, think about which resonates with you most and why. Ask yourself questions such as: What experiences do I have that will help me reach my goals? How much hard work am I willing to put in (Opportunity Costs)? Am I willing to invest in the training or education needed to get there? How do I balance my career goals with the other things that I love and are important to me (i.e., family, hobbies, self-care, etc.)? Answering these questions can help you gain clarity on your career goal and the potential paths you can take. You can then focus on taking actionable steps toward reaching your goals. It is important to remember that your goals may evolve over time, and that's okay! Make sure you check in with yourself regularly, and ask yourself, did you stay true to what brings you joy? Ultimately, this will give you the motivation needed to get there, stay there, and be successful.

You don't just want to make moves; you want to make the right moves—this is Chess, not Checkers. Taking time to define what you want to achieve will allow you to make more strategic moves throughout your professional life, and having a clear idea of where you want to take your career (what's your final destination) is essential for success. It allows you to set short-term and long-term goals that are tangible, achievable and should be rewarding. You want to have goals that will keep you motivated because, let's face it, the job market has more ups and downs than a rollercoaster and can be challenging at times. Having clarity on your career journey helps to build confidence as you focus on what you need to do to obtain your goals.

Also, let me state the obvious; having a clear understanding of where you are headed helps to reduce stress and anxiety by breaking the journey down into smaller, more manageable actions. Life is stressful enough without adding unnecessary stress into the system. Nobody has time for that.

Strategize Your Career

The definition of a tactic is "an action or strategy carefully planned to achieve a specific end." This is the premise of a great chess game (which I have eluded to) - maximize your strategy. As you do in chess, so you must do in corporate America. Intelligence is a great asset in the corporate space, but in addition to that, the most successful leaders also master deep thinking, prediction ability (reading the room/landscape), and, most importantly, tactical strategy.

A successful strategy formula for advancing your career is to continually strive to build connections and develop new skills. Networking with other professionals in your industry can open doors to potential job opportunities and ultimately help you move up the ladder. Additionally, stay up-to-date on trends in technology and leadership strategies; this will demonstrate that you are a proactive learner who is willing to adapt and grow. Ultimately, being prepared and taking the initiative are essential components of a successful career advancement strategy.

A well-defined career strategy involves shifting from a job-centered focus to a higher-level, more inclusive career outlook. This mindset shift reveals a clear destination and plan of action, ensuring you move like a Queen, not like a pawn, taking the right steps to reach your goals. Having a well-defined strategy will help you manage your time wisely, identify potential opportunities, stay organized, motivated, and find ways to overcome obstacles because you will encounter obstacles along this journey. Climbing the corporate ladder does have its thorns.

Your career strategy is dynamic and flexible. As you build your strategy, you need to consider what skills you currently possess, what future skills you require, and how you remain relevant and competitive in an ever-evolving market. Your strategy should not be stiff but adaptable and responsive to new input or feedback from the corporate environment and any new experiences you encounter. It needs to allow for changes and adjustments based on not only the current situation but potential opportunities. Visit **bonus.thefixbook.com** for a Career SWOT Worksheet and the Career Climbing Journal.

From Pawn to Queen

In chess, the pawn is often seen as the weakest piece on the board. It can only move forward one square at a time and cannot capture pieces directly. However, with some thoughtful maneuvering, a pawn can become a powerful queen. This transformation occurs when it reaches the opposite end of the board from where it started and can move in any direction. It is a great example of how something seemingly insignificant can become powerful when given the opportunity, determination, and the right circumstances.

A career plan for achieving promotion is a Venn diagram that melds your personal short and long-term goals with the company's needs. As you develop your plan, it is important to understand the org's culture, processes, and available resources (reading the chess board). This is accomplished by conducting research or meeting with key stakeholders. After gaining a better understanding of the organizational environment, developing clear goals and objectives can help align expectations in regard to performance and deliverables.

Let's say you join the company as an individual contributor, but your goal is to obtain the top executive position. You will need to have a plan to do so. Your plan may include strengthening current skills or gaining new skills required to get that position. In addition, you need to be able to answer these questions: Who is typically the person responsible for hiring for that position? Have you built a relationship with them? What are the core competencies needed to get the position? I help my clients identify opportunities, boost their determination and prepare to pivot and capitalize on the right circumstances so they are better positioned and on the radar for the desired promotions.

By taking a proactive approach, you will continue to set yourself up for potential advancement within your organization. In this way, a pawn can become a queen and so can YOU with the right plan!

Chapter 3 - Summary - Establishing a Blueprint:
- Build a Strong Foundation on Personal Values
- Be Honest With Yourself About Your Gaps
- Get Clear on Your Goals
- Be Strategic - This is Chess, not Checkers
- Transform Yourself From a Pawn to a Queen

Chapter 3 - Reflection: Establish a blueprint

What skill gaps are stalling your corporate climb?

_____

_____

_____

_____

_____

_____

_____

_____

_____

What is your ultimate career goal? Why?

_____

_____

_____

_____

_____

_____

_____

_____

_____

What adjustments need to be made to your career strategy?

_____

_____

_____

_____

_____

_____

_____

_____

_____

Be Intentional

"An unintentional life accepts everything and does nothing. An intentional life embraces only the things that will add to the mission of significance."

~ John C. Maxwell

I t's important to be intentional with your actions because otherwise, you can make missteps. You can be doing ALL the things and not do the RIGHT thing. So being focused and intentional about how you execute is absolutely essential.

Focused intentionality accomplishes two things. First - it identifies the right thing for YOU. Second - it helps others hold you accountable for doing the right things successfully in your journey to climbing the corporate ladder. As always, here are some questions you need to ask yourself: What relationships do I need to establish? What relationships do I need to nourish and maintain? What relationships do I need to eliminate? Yes, this means your raggedy-arse friends, you know exactly who they are already. What things are not serving me any longer, or what things have never really served me?

So really take the time to inventory the actions required to support the execution of your blueprint. I've had lots of missteps in my 30-plus-year career because I didn't know ANY of these things, not one. And the reality is, once you know better, you do better. I've learned along the way and have the scars to prove it. And the goal here is to ensure that you don't make the same mistakes but have the opportunity to gain focused, meaningful experiences.

Say Yes to Opportunities

Saying "Yes" to new opportunities is an important part of life. It opens up possibilities and helps you grow as a person. When you say yes, it can open doors that would have otherwise stayed closed—both in terms of career advancement and personal growth. Saying yes also shows a willingness to take risks, which employers highly value. When you say yes, it allows you to meet new people and experience new things outside your comfort zone, which can lead to unexpected rewards. By taking on challenges and stepping out of your routine, you push yourself further than ever, leading toward success. Therefore, if presented with a new opportunity or challenge, don't hesitate to say "yes." You never know what could come from it!

To be successful, everything starts with believing in yourself, now and forever, without apology. Believing is so much more potent than it seems at first glance. Believing is committing to an unshakable confidence in yourself that thrives even in chaos. It is a muscle you must exercise to perfect. It's not about proving you belong there; it's about knowing you belong there and that you already have everything you need. You didn't get to where you are by mistake, right? A lot of times, we erroneously question our capabilities and create self-doubt. Whatever your challenge, have the mindset that you will make it your Bytch!

Have you ever let someone else tell you what you could or couldn't do? And then you believed them more than you believed in yourself? Maybe it was society, a colleague at work, your boss's boss, family, friends, your spouse, or your girlfriends—you know, the raggedy ones you meet for happy hour or brunch to swap your miserable work stories. How dare you think you can get a promotion? How dare you think you should go for the promotion? Girl, they're not gonna give you the job.

You might be saying - well, your raggedy friends are just jealous, but surely your family would support you in your "yes" moments. However, for me, sometimes the most well-meaning family members, the people closest to you, don't always support or share your vision. My story starts in my hometown, Wisconsin. For those that know anything about Wisconsin, it is a cold place, and it was not a place that I truly enjoyed. To be honest, I felt like I was switched at birth (LOL!) because I really hated the cold. I spent most of my life and career living and working in Wisconsin. It wasn't until I personally made the decision that I was going to pursue an opportunity that was going to get me out of Wisconsin that things changed.

Every time I pursued an out-of-state opportunity, it really would not come to fruition. One day a headhunter found and contacted me about an opportunity. I was so excited as I told my family and friends about the opportunity, expecting them to be excited with me and for me. However, all they had for me was, "it's not going work out," "you need to stay here and wait until the kids finish school," "your father-in-law is battling cancer," "your husband is scheduled for knee replacement surgery," and and and... Everybody had a reason why I shouldn't pursue it, and I could have responded to the headhunter that now is not the right time, very easily returning to my routine.

A pivotal moment occurred when my girlfriend, JAG, called. She's the girlfriend who will tell you what you need to hear, not what you want to hear. Every one of us should have a JAG. She said, "it's not every day somebody finds you for an opportunity that you weren't even looking for. How do you know this isn't God's way of telling you this is the right time." Amid all the chaos, God air-dropped an opportunity in a way only He could. So during the challenging circumstances mentioned above, and people validating that those challenges should drive me to stay put, I took the risk and said "YES" to the opportunity. If I had listened and believed those around me, allowing them and my circumstances to derail my faith and self-belief, I would not be where I am in my career today. So, saying YES to opportunities (i.e., stretch assignments, audacious situations, challenging customers, etc.) is my favorite thing to do, and it has served me well over my career journey.

Having the Right Mindset

Over the course of my career, I've had many leaders that I've worked for, but there is one that stays in the forefront of my mind, although when working for her, I went home almost daily in tears and wanted nothing more than to quit. But let's be real...my bills were not going to pay for themselves, and there were no indecent proposals on the horizon…LOL! Once I convinced my husband to let me quit, I had a sense of peace going into the office that day. When I met with her to resign, she shocked me by refusing to accept my resignation. She shared that I had promise and that I was not fully aware of the greatness that resided inside me, and she pushed me as she did because I was operating as if I was just like everyone else and I was not "average" by any stretch. She asked that I go home and think about what she had said, and if I still wanted to quit tomorrow, she would accept my resignation. But if I had a change of heart, we would get to work leaning into the hard stuff because my growth was on the other side of it. She was my first unofficial coach and was pivotal in helping me shift from a job-centric view to a career mindset. She taught me the importance of establishing a blueprint, having a strategy for my career, and how to create and execute a plan.

That experience helped me understand that having the right mindset is an essential asset for advancing your career. "As a woman thinks, so she is"—the world, according to Dana. I've found that having a positive and growth-oriented mindset helps you stay motivated, take risks and step outside of your comfort zone as you take advantage of opportunities.

In tandem with developing and growing in the right mindset, one has to also be open and stay coachable to successfully progress through the level of your career. With the right mindset, you can conquer any obstacle that comes your way on the climb up. Ultimately, having the right mindset can be one of the most powerful tools in advancing your career...because where the mind goes, your life follows.

I'm sure I'm not the only one who has failed to show up as my authentic self because my mindset was not in the right place. I don't have many peers that look like me in similar positions, but I do have one, and we often speak about some of the challenges that we encounter. For example, when walking into a room full of people that are not like us, whether it's because of ethnicity or gender, and what we think about in those situations. Often when I walk into a room and I survey the audience, my initial thoughts are immediately about me and NOT what I'm there to do. I'm thinking, "Darn, I'm the only black person or woman in the room," and if I'm focused on that, what am I not thinking about?

It boils down to this—as you think, so you are, or so you become. As you're thinking, "They are not going to listen to me," or "They are not going to see me as valuable to this conversation," or "They are not going to respond to my questions," your thought process is one of defeat, and you begin to decline. The way you are presenting and representing them aligns with your thoughts, it manifests in your actions, and it becomes a forgone conclusion. This jaded conclusion turns into a truth that wasn't the truth to begin with. I'm sure I'm not the only one that has dealt with this.

For me, it came down to a paradigm shift in my thinking; that shift occurred with daily affirmations. My coach challenged me to stand in front of the mirror and look at my face and say affirmations directly to my innermost being. Once I started doing this, it affected how I saw myself and transformed how I showed up and how others experienced me.

Daily affirmation in the mirror is a way of life. It is one of the most powerful things I've ever experienced. It's a way to train your mind not to think about the dynamics you face but to think about the value you bring. I firmly believe that where the mind goes, the body and life follow. We create our truth and set the energy in the rooms we enter.

Many of us walk into these rooms with the thought process that we have to prove ourselves to these people when the reality is you just have to believe you deserve to be exactly where you are at that moment. Your mindset should be, "I wouldn't be here if I weren't equipped." I have complete and total faith that the God I serve puts me in spaces and places that He has already prepared for me and me for them. Visit **bonus.thefixbook.com** for Affirmation Cards to shift your mindset.

Balancing Act

Life is all about balance. While striving for career advancement and personal growth, it's equally important to maintain a healthy work-life balance that allows you to enjoy your life beyond the workplace. This includes time for friends and family, leisure activities, hobbies, and self-care. To achieve the perfect balance between work and life, set boundaries with yourself and your employer, prioritize rest when needed, take your vacation, schedule regular breaks from work tasks throughout the day or week, take advantage of flexible working hours if available, delegate tasks when possible, and practice self-discipline as well as self-care. With an appropriate amount of dedication and planning, you can enjoy success in your professional life while still having enough energy to appreciate all that life has to offer.

By taking the time to develop a balance between work and leisure, you will help ensure that your career can thrive while helping you live a more meaningful life outside of the workplace. With this balanced approach, you will benefit from both aspects of life—achieving success at work while having time for family, friends, hobbies, and self-care. Ultimately, it's important to remember that when it comes to balancing career advancement with personal happiness, there is no one-size-fits-all solution for everyone—just strive for a healthy balance that works best for you!

Climbing the corporate ladder can be a stressful and demanding endeavor. It is important to prioritize self-care and maintain a healthy balance between work and home life. Taking regular breaks, exercising, eating nutritious meals, sleeping well, and engaging in activities that bring joy are all essential components of taking good care of oneself on the journey up the corporate ladder. Self-care helps keep stress levels in check while helping you stay focused on the tasks at hand. In addition to physical health needs, it's just as important to nurture mental health when climbing the corporate ladder. Making time for hobbies or engaging in meaningful conversations with friends and family are great ways to de-stress and reconnect with your values outside work. While it may feel like there is no time for self-care, it's essential to make it a priority to keep your energy and motivation high as you strive for success. Self-care can be the difference between achieving professional goals or getting derailed by stress. By taking care of oneself along the way, one can climb higher up the corporate ladder with greater peace of mind and satisfaction.

It's not about what has worked for anyone else. It's about the self-care formula that works for me. Once I discovered it, there was no stopping me because I knew who I was. I know how to lead in a room full of leaders. I know how to show up and be present. I also know how to take care of myself to keep that going. One of the things leaders fall down on is self-care. We have to be in a very solid and good place mentally to lead others.

I can't serve you well if I'm unhappy, not taking care of myself, or if I have deficiencies and gaps in my life that I'm trying to address. If I'm distracted, I cannot meet the needs of those I lead because I'm so focused on my chaos—on my ISH.

Really good leaders know what they need to do to be at their optimal performance daily. A few great examples are Jeff Bezos, founder and executive chairman of Amazon, and Marc Randolph, co-founder and first CEO of Netflix. Jeff Bezos doesn't take meetings before 10 o'clock or after 5 o'clock because he knows the importance of thinking and preparing himself for his day. Marc Randolph talks about working hard his entire career to keep his life balanced with his job and how he held Tuesdays sacred for date night with his wife and left faithfully by 5 o'clock. Having the clarity to know what you need to perform at your best and the discipline to align your values with your work will keep things in the proper perspective.

In conclusion, balance is an essential part of the journey up the corporate ladder. Taking time to prioritize physical and mental health needs can help reduce stress and keep motivation high.

Be A Lifelong Learner

As long as there is breath in my lungs, I believe I owe it to myself to stay on top of what's happening in my industry and to ensure that I stay competitive in the marketplace. That, however, requires a willingness to learn. Many of us high-achieving, driven women have had to overcome many things in life, most of which we did by forging our path and being self-reliant, independent, and headstrong.

All of these are powerful traits until they are NOT. When you get to the place where you fail to read the tea leaves of your life, your career journey, or both are trying to tell you, then Houston, we have a problem.

I'm not sure how strong your head is, but I'm certain it can't withstand too many blows against the brick wall of "career stagnation." It's in these moments that you need to be not only flexible but willing to learn the lessons necessary to move forward. Practical experience and tribal knowledge definitely go a long way in advancing your career, as well as other things that aren't necessarily learned in a classroom, book, or seminar, like soft skills (e.g., time management, communication, adaptability, interpersonal skills, etc.).

I am not diminishing the value of advanced degrees or certifications, as having these assets can propel your career, displaying you have the education and knowledge needed to take on more complex challenges and responsibilities. So if you are going to get a degree or certification, get it in something that will make you happy, NOT because it seems like the right thing to do or feels like something you "should" do. If it doesn't bring you joy, then it doesn't make sense.

Network Wisely

A sponsor, mentor, and coach are all essential components to successfully climbing the corporate ladder. A sponsor who influences the company and can help open doors by leveraging their corporate currency is a powerful advocate for you. Having a sponsor who is willing to promote you, endorse your work, and advocate for you within the organization can be an invaluable asset. They are someone who will champion your cause, provide introductions to key decision makers, help you chart out a winning career plan, and provide honest feedback to help keep you on track. A mentor who can provide guidance and wisdom from their personal experiences can be invaluable for helping you navigate tricky professional situations. Finally, a coach will help you identify areas of improvement and develop strategies for achieving your career goals. Having a mentor, a sponsor, and a coach can create powerful momentum in achieving personal and professional success. It's important to take the initiative to find a sponsor, mentor, and coach that can help guide you through challenging career decisions or growth opportunities so that you can reach your professional goals faster.

This type of support is challenging to achieve and requires a great deal of commitment and hard work. Take the time to invest in relationships that can help you reach your goals and foster meaningful connections with potential sponsors. Doing so will help you leverage all available resources to maximize your career trajectory.

Manage your sponsorship with care—everything does not require a hammer. At the same time, it's important to recognize that a sponsor may not be an appropriate fit for everyone or every situation, so it's wise to carefully evaluate any potential relationship before entering into one. Be sure to conduct due diligence as needed and clearly define expectations up front to create a successful sponsorship opportunity for both parties involved.

Overall, having a dedicated sponsor, a mentor, and the right coach can provide invaluable support and guidance when exploring new opportunities or making important career decisions, making it an essential element to advancing your career. Take the time to find and cultivate relationships with your potential support system to capitalize on their expertise as you progress in your professional journey.

Chapter 4 - Summary - Being Intentional:

- Say "Yes" to Opportunities - Your Growth is on the Other Side
- Manage Your Mindset Towards Positivity and Growth
- Prioritize Balance in Life - You Only Have One Life to Live!
- Always Be Open to Learning
- Select and Leverage Your Support System Wisely

Chapter 4 - Reflection: Be Intentional

What is an opportunity you didn't say yes to? What stopped you?

_____

_____

_____

_____

_____

_____

_____

_____

What am I saying or doing to myself that is holding me back and impacting my mindset?

_____

_____

_____

_____

_____

_____

_____

_____

Do you think you have a healthy balance between life and work? If not, how can you improve it?

_____

_____

_____

_____

_____

_____

_____

_____

_____

What are your thoughts telling you about how successful you might be at learning something new? If these thoughts are limiting to me, how might I think differently?

_____

_____

_____

_____

_____

_____

_____

_____

_____

Don't be afraid to be different

"Always remember that you are absolutely unique.
Just like everyone else."
~ Maya Angelou

Whon looking to climb the corporate ladder, it can be tempting to try to fit in and do what everyone else is doing. Please don't make that mistake. Standing out for being different can actually be an advantage when striving for success. Being unique and taking on different approaches often brings fresh perspectives that are invaluable to any organization. Embracing your authentic self allows you to showcase your individuality and stand out from your peers by demonstrating your creativity and resourcefulness. Finally, having the courage to move outside of your comfort zone can open up more opportunities for advancement and help build relationships that can prove incredibly valuable on your journey. In this way, not being afraid to be different is essential when looking to make a lasting impact in the workplace.

Be Allergic to Average

If you're looking to climb the corporate ladder, it is important to stand out from the rest. Standing out will demonstrate your abilities and skills that make you a valuable asset to any company. It could be through showing initiative, taking on more responsibility than expected, or demonstrating an ability to think outside of the box. Doing so will showcase your unique quality and help you get noticed by leadership when opportunities arise. Additionally, having a strong network of colleagues who can vouch for your capabilities and support you in pursuing higher positions can give you a competitive edge over others vying for the same roles.

Ultimately standing out is essential if you want to make progress in climbing up the corporate ladder. One thing I tell myself is to be certain that I make my presence known and my absence felt. This is my daily mantra everywhere I show up. What's top of mind for you when you show up? Are you the type of person who keeps your head down and does a good job with the hopes that one day someone will recognize your efforts? Or are you the person who is standing out from the crowd, who is allergic to average, living out loud while raising your hand? I like to use the phrase: Use the ABCs (Always Be Curious). Always staying curious means continuously questioning the status quo and discovering ways to be innovative. You are always challenging yourself with the intention of improving the process, the team, and/or the value that you and your organization are bringing to the other parts of the organization or your customers on the back end. Good is not a destination for you—Greater is always in sight.

Delivery Matters

Average people who are comfortable with good deliver to expectations. Exceptional people who aspire to greatness? They deliver more than is expected, or as we say in corporate, they exceed expectations. To be clear, the average is not a bad thing; it's delivering results consistently. Consistent delivery demonstrates your competence, credibility, and trustworthiness to superiors, colleagues, and customers; and builds a reputation for reliability and dependability that will open up more opportunities for advancement and growth. Consequently, it is important to develop strategies for ensuring that results are delivered reliably and efficiently. This can include setting achievable deadlines, breaking projects into manageable chunks, communicating progress regularly with stakeholders, and utilizing available resources effectively. By continuously delivering successful results, you become an invaluable asset to your organization or team and set yourself up for even greater success in the future.

Delivering more than expected is an important part of climbing the corporate ladder because when you repeatedly exceed expectations, it shows your superiors that you are willing to go above and beyond the call of duty, demonstrating a level of commitment and dedication that is worthy of reward and promotion. It also allows you to distinguish yourself from others in the workplace by showing off your creativity, resourcefulness, and problem-solving skills. Going above and beyond helps build trust between yourself and those around you, enabling more opportunities for collaboration with colleagues and other departments within the organization. In this way, delivering more than expected is essential for anyone looking to advance their career in a meaningful way.

Ultimately, performing in this way allows you to stand out while building a strong foundation for long-term success. It creates a positive feedback loop that reinforces the skills and knowledge needed to achieve great things while demonstrating your commitment to excellence. In this way, delivering results is one of the most important steps to achieving lasting success in any career or profession.

Let your work make all the noise

When climbing the corporate ladder, it is essential to let your "receipts" of success make all the noise. Not letting pride get in the way of progress is a key trait that leaders look for when hiring and promoting. Focus on achieving tangible results that speak volumes about your capabilities, whether it's through improving processes, delivering successful projects, or setting new standards in service. Letting your success do the talking can quickly help you climb up the ranks and reach higher levels of responsibility. Please don't take this to mean that you should not be evangelizing your work because you most certainly should *(see The Story of You)*.

Evangelizing your body of work is an important part of the process because it allows you to showcase your accomplishments and demonstrate how you contribute to the organization. Talking about your portfolio of work not only gets others excited about what you are doing, but you create visibility for yourself and opportunities for collaboration on projects that can result in big wins for you, others, and the organization. As you evangelize your work, it also helps build relationships within the workplace which can truly be an invaluable way to expand your network when looking to advance your career.

Don't get me wrong, your network can be a very powerful tool, but your network can change —people come and go; however, the one thing that no one can take away from you is your "Receipts." #FACTS!

Embrace your differences

Personally, I've spent years figuring out which lane I belonged in; was it this lane or that lane? People told me the lane they thought I should be in, but nothing felt right. Those lanes weren't for me because I am fearfully and wonderfully made. I am a CUSTOM design. My personality, my dreams, what irritates me, what motivates me, and my purpose are UNIQUE. I am the LANE! I am meant for MY purpose, as you are for yours. Stop trying to fit into a lane. Stop allowing others to box you in. Stop prioritizing the comfort of others above what makes you GREAT. You are designed for YOUR purpose. Everything about you is UNIQUE! EMBRACE IT! If you don't, no one else will.

You can always reach the top of any ladder if you know how to embrace and use your differences. Truly great leaders have this ability, and it's what makes them successful. So embrace your differences and let your uniqueness shine through so that you will be noticed by those in authority who can help you succeed. There is no one on this earth like you. You are unique; that is a value-add all by itself. If you think about it, the mold was broken the moment you were created, and that, to me, is PRICELESS. Be proud of what makes you different because it might propel you above others. It's okay to stand out! So go ahead and embrace your uniqueness, for there are no two alike on this planet! You got this!

Chapter 5 - Summary - Don't Be Afraid to Be Different:
- Don't Be Mediocre - Status Quo is a NO!
- Meet or Exceed Expectations, but be Consistent
- Let Your Receipts Show How Great You Are
- Accept and Honor the Uniqueness of You

Chapter 5 - Reflection: Don't be Afraid to be Different

How are you showing up - Are you blending in or standing out? Do you know where you have the opportunity to exceed expectations?

_____

_____

_____

_____

_____

_____

_____

_____

_____

List your top 5 accomplishments. How can you leverage these accomplishments to tell your story of you?

_____

_____

_____

_____

_____

_____

_____

_____

What makes you unique? How can you use this uniqueness more?

_____

_____

_____

_____

_____

_____

_____

_____

_____

SECTION 3

THE EXECUTION

CHAPTER 6

Do I Need a Coach?

"A coach is someone who tells you what you don't want
to hear, who has you see what you don't want to see,
so you can be who you have always known
you could be."
~Tom Landry

I t is important to know and realize that the coach is not the one to do the work. YOU will have to do the work. You're wondering why you should hire a coach? A coach is a key part of that support system. The role that the coach plays is one of connection. They help you find the connection, help you build confidence, and help you to develop your unrealized, untapped potential. That's why you should hire a coach.

Some people plant in your life. Other people water. Coaches help you harvest. Specifically, coaches help you harvest the diamonds that are buried in your garden. Coaches help you harvest the diamonds that are buried in your backyard. They help you find them, mine them and clean them up until they sparkle. In case you are wondering, YES, pressure is involved. They didn't plant anything—they just helped you find what was already there.

I've had several coaches during my career journey at different intervals. Heck - I have a coach now! I have a few coaches now. Each of them has been beneficial in their areas of strength by providing the guidance and insights I needed. When I mention this to most people, they look at me in a state of confusion. Their response is usually, "Well, you're successful and already a senior-level executive at a Fortune 500 company. Why do you need a coach?" There were things I needed to refine. I also had come to a place in my life where I had reached a point that I had never been at before. My own personal foundation was rocked by tragedies that had occurred over the course of several years due to Covid and other life challenges. I know I'm not the only person who has had this experience, especially during Covid. My coaches have been instrumental in being a sounding board for my thought processes, challenging me to move out of what is comfortable and into the uncomfortable. Even I need a reminder to be comfortable with being uncomfortable.

One of the things I have carried into my own practice that I gleaned from my coaches is that while success in your career is a great end result, that is not the source of my true joy or my true North. All your areas impact each other—you can't compartmentalize the facets of your life.

Finding the right coach

Finding the right coach is like finding the right mate; you can't just marry the first person that comes along. Well, you can, but then you are playing a game of risk. Working with a coach who understands and believes in you can provide much-needed encouragement, support, and guidance so that you can reach your personal and professional goals. You want someone who has a personality and temperament that resonates with you. A good coach will challenge you to think outside of the box, identify opportunities or changes that are needed to help you move forward, they will ask you the right combination of thought-provoking questions, and provide tailored advice and strategies to help maximize your success. Finding someone who has expertise in the areas relevant to your aspirations is important as they will be better able to give you informed advice on how best to achieve them. Ultimately, selecting the right coach will not only help you reach your desired outcomes but also empower you with confidence and the skills needed for ongoing success.

Additionally, you may want to consider asking yourself what your expectations and desired outcomes are from working with a coach. Having a clear understanding of this can help you select the right coach that can best guide, challenge, and support you in achieving your goals. This kind of investment should not be taken lightly, so take your time when selecting the right coach for you.

What to expect when working with a coach

When working with a coach, expect to gain greater clarity on your career direction and set attainable goals to help you achieve your desired outcomes. You can also expect to develop self-awareness, build the skills needed for success, and create an actionable plan that is tailored specifically to you because one size does not fit all. You should also expect to receive feedback that can aid you in improving your performance and uncovering areas of development. The best part is, working with a coach will provide accountability and structure so that you can stay focused and motivated throughout your corporate ladder climb. Ultimately, if you select the right coach, success is within your reach, so make sure to invest the time and effort needed to find the best one for you.

Testimonial - Aleeta Gardner

"Dana is one of the most authentic and transparent people I have ever met, making my coaching experience with her enjoyable and effective. Dana wants you first to know that you are enough. She pulled out my strengths that were already there that I didn't recognize existed and taught me that the words I use to speak about and define myself matter. Dana has taught me to say yes to opportunities and the world seemed to open up to me. After working with Dana, I realized if you plan and strategize, you can have it all."

Testimonial - Luceanne Welge

"Dana has been a mentor/coach to me as I made the transition from early to experienced professional. Working under Dana's tutelage has given me the confidence and support I needed to uncover my strengths, reach my goals, and continually refine and reassess my career path. Dana's emphasis on showing up "consistently" and focusing on the "right" things have made all the difference in my professional development. It truly makes you realize that some of

the most impactful things (i.e., showing up on time, doing what you say you'll do, treating others with kindness, and being yourself) are free of cost. Dana helps you to see the bigger picture and strategically identify all stakeholders at the proverbial "table." She also helps you develop plans for how you can forge meaningful and mutually beneficial relationships with each individual stakeholder, whether they are employees, peers, or superiors. I can't endorse Dana enough for those looking for an experienced, honest, and empathetic coach who has navigated the corporate waters with proven success."

What criteria to use to know if you are ready for a coach

So one of the ways to know you are ready for a coach is you realize what made you successful as an individual contributor won't necessarily make you successful as a leader. Also, if you feel stuck in your current career and don't know how to move forward, it may be time to look into hiring a coach. Other signs that you are ready for a coach include feeling overwhelmed by the job search process, having difficulty setting goals for yourself, or wanting to make a big change but not knowing where to start.

A coach can help provide clarity and direction so that you can make the best decisions for your professional future. A coach can also provide valuable advice and guidance on how to identify opportunities, develop strategies for success, and land meaningful roles with employers who share your values. Working with the right coach can help you gain confidence, realize your potential, and reach your career goals. If any of these signs sound familiar, it may be time to invest in a coach and take your career to the next level. With the right guidance, you can gain valuable insights that will help you reach your professional goals. So don't hesitate if you're ready for a change or want to make sure you're on the right track with your current career; it may be time to consider hiring a coach.

Chapter 6 - Reflection: Do I Need A Coach?

Who is on your support team? Are there any adjustments/changes you need to make to optimize your climb?

_____

_____

_____

_____

_____

_____

_____

_____

_____

_____

_____

_____

_____

Do you have the right people on your team for this season you are in? ☐Y ☐N

Does your team align with your goals? ☐Y ☐N

Does your team have the expertise to assist in your climb? ☐Y ☐N

If you answered NO to any of the above, list three actions you can take.

_____

_____

_____

_____

_____

_____

_____

_____

Who will hold you accountable?

_____

_____

_____

_____

_____

_____

_____

_____

Chapter 7

Take Charge

"It is only when you take responsibility
for your life that you discover how powerful
you truly are."

~ Allanah Hunt

To be a successful woman leader, you must first believe in yourself and that the future is bright. *"The future's so bright, I gotta wear shades!"* Remember that song by Timbuk3? Maybe I'm dating myself…LOL! Is there a bright future for Women in Leadership? Yes! Without a doubt! Leadership is about facing constant challenges, building, innovating, stabilizing teams, triumphing over obstacles, and never having the same day twice. Whew!

For those who have accepted the challenge and are wearing their shades for their really bright futures, the essential steps are: take charge of your career, obtain an understanding of the professional landscape and clarify the steps to reach your goals. All of these activities will help foster growth, success, and satisfaction. Through planning and goal-setting, it's possible to create a well-defined career path that gives you control over your own destiny and allows you to make decisions based on what you value most rather than solely relying on outside influences.

The Female Quotient (FQ)

As more organizations recognize the value of diversity and inclusion in the workplace, there has been an increase in the number of women that are being appointed to top leadership positions within businesses. The Female Quotient or the value add delivered as a direct correlation to an increased female presence, is a real phenomenon that more companies are capitalizing on. Female leaders bring a unique set of experiences and perspectives, which can be incredibly beneficial for any organization looking to create an environment where different ideas can thrive. An unprecedented opportunity has evolved for leaders like you and me, who are ambitious and driven to make meaningful contributions while inspiring others to pursue their own paths toward success. Organizations greatly benefit from creating an environment where different prospectives can thrive. It is clear that women are increasingly being recognized for their accomplishments and hard work globally, which allows us to take advantage of the opportunity to shape our futures, so not only is our future bright, but it's full of potential.

The 7 Biggest Lessons to Execute The F.I.X.

Here are 7 of the BIGGEST LESSONS I want you all to learn as women leaders with bright futures:

1. **Game On! Playing the Game of Leadership**
   Leadership is a game, and as they say in chess, it's time to make your opening move. If you are on the board but not making moves, you are at risk for capture. In other words, play the game or be played! You decide how you show up and present yourself, so show up confidently. DO NOT ever quit when it comes to getting what you desire, and

also recognize that if something is not working, stop putting more energy into it. Own your board.

2. **In a World of Fake, Keep It Real**

   Are people meeting and experiencing the real you or your representative? Do you know who the real you is? As the world changes, we see that people are starting to have honest conversations about authenticity and being able to trust others. Show others who you are. Are you funny and detail-oriented? Do you support others openly? Can you hold someone's confidence? Do you demonstrate empathy? Are you comfortable being uncomfortable? Show the world who you are and that uniqueness still has a place in this world.

3. **Get Clear on Your Desire: Pursue this RUTH-LESSLY**

   Only you know what you want out of this life, and your imagination only limits what you seek to achieve. Once you spend time getting to know yourself and nurturing your inner self, I recommend spending time getting clear about what it is YOU want. Don't limit this to just career, ladies. It's time to start designing your dream life! A career is one piece of that puzzle. Weak desires bring weak results and inspire confidence in no one!

4. **Be the Queen Bee, not the Worker Bee.**

   Don't be just a Worker Bee! True leaders do not bury their heads in work or data. Leaders stay open to possibilities in seeing trends and changes in the marketplace. She keeps the pulse, maintains boots on the ground, asks fundamental questions, and opens others up to what the market is missing. Become social in a unique way and engage others as only you can. Show yourself and stand in your power and demand the light and shine bright! Others need to see you, hear you, and know you RIGHT NOW!

5. **Dream BIG, Ask BIGGER**

   Don't put your dreams and goals on hold for ANYONE, not even you! In an age of monkeypox, pandemic, inflation, and supposed recession, what are you waiting for? Tomorrow is not promised! Get yours now. Who do you need to be around? Where else can you express and demonstrate your zone of genius? Please don't delay; write it out and make it plain. Execute! Ask others for help and gain their attention and respect in the process. Most people do not ask and do not get further in their careers. And while asking, Ask BIGGER of yourself and everyone around you!

6. **Chase Your Dreams and Secure the BHAG that Reflects Your Worth!**

   Make sure you are treating yourself as if you are already worthy! Examine if your paycheck reflects this fact. If it does not, as a leader, you will have to make hard decisions, and one may be to put yourself out there more to get what you need. To stay on the radar of others who make those decisions and have those decisions be in your favor every time.

7. **Find Your Tribe**
   - Now, I'm not talking about your raggedy friends who listen to you complain and bond over mutual trauma.
   - You need a group of women who will PUSH you to be better and support you along your journey. There is a lot of brokenness in this world, and the last thing you need is someone to validate your misery without pushing you to be better.
   - Reset your mind and find your tribe. These women are out there.
   - Happiness and positivity attract money, promotions, referrals, and other opportunities!
   - Start weeding and pruning NOW! Your ability to soar as a leader comes from being around

other leaders, not followers or those who accept their fate.

From Doing to Being

"A waterfall is concerned only with being itself, not with doing something it considers waterfall-like."

~ Vernon Howard

As we end, I would like to leave you with one of the best pieces of advice I have ever received from another fantastic woman leader who genuinely impacted my life.

"We get this one short life to live, and you get to determine if you make an impact or not. Life is short and unpredictable. No one will permit you to be happy, free, and healthy. That is YOUR responsibility." ~ Christy Rutherford

Focus more on BEING who you are AUTHENTICALLY in all situations and less on DOING what you think is expected. Everyone will BENEFIT from experiencing YOU in your FULLNESS.

I genuinely believe there is endless potential and strength for women leaders right now if we only embrace the unique gifts we have to offer. I hope you do too. Here's to women being the bright future ahead and taking their rightful place.

Listen, leadership is so NOT easy, no matter who tells you it is! You may want a social media life, yet it takes hard work and being a leader means you are out front. Will you make mistakes? Heck yes! Those who risk something achieve something.

So, leadership is not about all the degrees from fancy schools (no hate), certifications, or more courses or charity work. Stand out by BEING you! Do what brings you joy. Show who YOU are. Invite yourself to where the power players are. Show them what they are missing and call checkmate!

Conclusion

The journey up the corporate ladder can be challenging, but it doesn't have to be. With dedication, hard work, and the right team you can overcome any obstacle in your way. I discovered where I was in life was not my final destination. I found there is greater in me and for me. I realized where I started was never where I was intended to finish.

To get to the next level, I had to be willing to transform. Understanding that accepting what I was not ready to change would only keep me stuck. It was time to move forward. While seasons change with time, my life would only change when I did.

The same is true for you. What God has for you can not be stopped. Rise and start speaking life over everything in your environment. You are the catalyst. You are the change.

Speak to your vision rather than your circumstances. Be so bold as to declare the Glory of God and watch Him work.

Your value is PRICELESS, your potential is LIMITLESS, and when you finally see what God sees in you, you will be UNSTOPPABLE, just like me.

I am committed to helping successful professionals reach their next level of professional and personal success. Whether it's developing a strategy for career advancement, overcoming challenges in the workplace, or improving performance, my goal is to provide tailored solutions and strategies that help drive results. If you're feeling stuck or overwhelmed, or are seeking to reach your full potential, I'd be honored to help you get there.

The steps outlined in this book are not easy to accomplish, but I am here to help you along your journey with the tools and guidance. How you move forward is entirely up to you, but I'm certain my program can help. Are you ready to climb? If so, visit **bonus.thefixbook. com** to strap up for the journey toward achieving your goals. Together, we can make it happen!

Business Listings

Jacqueline "JaQ" Campbell
President, CEO, & Senior Wealth Advisor
Office: 248.209.3698 | Toll-Free: 877.206.6556
Fax 248.209.3696

Alexander Legacy Private Wealth Management
400 Renaissance Center Drive #2600
Detroit, MI 48243
www.alprivatewealth.com

Jacqueline "JaQ" Campbell leads Alexander Legacy Private Wealth as President, CEO and Senior Wealth Advisor.

Jacqueline's professional background began in 1993 as a high school intern for Comerica's Private Bank in Southfield, MI. She ascended from high school intern to running a $1.8 billion investment team for Chase Wealth Management, and now leads Alexander Legacy Private Wealth Management, as Founder and CEO, where her mission is to advance the next generation of advisors and investors in wealth management.

Jaq's passion for the community extends to her service on multiple boards and organizations that focus on driving impact around diversity and inclusion and financial independence. She has worked closely with organizations and business resource groups, such as Year Up, Financial Services Pipeline, LoveJoy Special Needs Center, amongst many other volunteer efforts targeting churches, sororities, and other community organizations.

Jaq holds her bachelor's degree in Liberal Arts with a focus area on Diverse Leadership in Financial Services from DePaul University. She also holds her Series 63 & 65 securities registrations.

Jaq's passion is being a "MIP" Mother, Innovator and Philanthropist.

As a mother to two beautiful children, Austin and Taylor Dion 'TD', she is constantly inspired by them to operate in her true calling and purpose. As an innovator, Jaq enjoys thinking outside the box and blazing new trails as a visionary and a problem solver. As a philanthropist, Jaq's philosophy is to give, save, then spend to win, win, win, because if you do the first two, they will always take care of you!

Follow Jacqueline "JaQ" Campbell on LinkedIn: https://www.linkedin.com/in/jaqcampbell
Follow Alexander Legacy Private Wealth Management:
https://www.linkedin.com/company/alexander-legacy-private-wealth-management/

Ngozi Okaro
Founder & Executive Director, Custom Collaborative

Ngozi Okaro advocates for a fashion industry that honors planet and people. She founded Custom Collaborative to support immigrant & no/low-income women launching sustainable fashion businesses and careers. Custom Collaborative serves fashion-industry entrepreneurs, workers, and consumers who value ethical fashion. Ngozi is a Commissioner of the NYC Equal Employment Practices Commission, and a Director of the NYC Economic Development Corporation. Among other honors, she is a 2022 Goldman Sachs Black Woman Impact Leader, Vogue Business 100 Innovator, and Conscious Fashion Campaign & United Nations SDG Honoree; 2021 AARP Purpose Prize Fellow, and Crain's Notable Woman in Business; 2020 "World-Changing Women in Conscious Business" winner, from Conscious Company Media and Kate Spade; 2019 NYC Fair Trade Coalition "Changemaker of the Year", and New York Women's Foundation "Spirit of Entrepreneurship" awardee. She is certified by New York University's Center for Philanthropy and Fundraising and was a 2014 Environmental Leadership Program Fellow. Ngozi graduated from Georgetown University Law Center and Morgan State University.

Follow Ngozi on Instagram, Twitter, ad LinkedIn:
IG: the.ngozi.okaro
TW: @NgoziOkaro
Linkedin: https://www.linkedin.com/in/ngoziokaro/

About Custom Collaborative
Vision: Custom Collaborative envisions a world in which all women possess the skills, confidence, and agency to design their futures and contribute to a sustainable world — regardless of race or socio-economic background.
Mission: Custom Collaborative trains, mentors, and advocates for and with no/low-income and immigrant women to build the skills necessary to achieve economic success in the sustainable fashion industry and broader society.

Follow Custom Collaborative on Twitter, Instagram, Facebook, YouTube, and LinkedIn:
Twitter and IG: @customcolab,
FB and Youtube: @customcollaborative
Linkedin: https://www.linkedin.com/company/custom-collaborative/

Crystle Johnson
Founder & CXO, The DEI Coach

Crystle Johnson is a data driven, organizational architect who leverages equitable process design to create spaces where underestimated talent can grow and thrive. Going beyond traditional, superficial means, she is laser-focused on building relationships across diverse communities, intentional career pathing, sponsorship, and removing barriers in everyday processes.

Crystle has several years of experience in the DEI space and as a Black woman, intimately understands how easily doing and being the work can lead to burnout. She founded The DEI Coach to create a space for Black women who serve as DEI professionals, as she understands first hand to DO and BE the work, leads to stress, burnout, and the loss of YOU. So, she's creating curated spaces where Black women can show up authentically, cultivate community, and thrive through self-care and rest. Spaces where Black women are expected, respected, valued, and fully centered.

Crystle has been Quoted & Seen In: Forbes, SHRM HR Magazine, Professional Woman's Magazine (Wonder Woman edition), Living Corporate Podcast, xoNecole, Medium

Follow Crystle Johnson on LinkedIn: linkedin.com/in/thedeicoach
Follow The DEI Coach on Instagram: https://www.instagram.com/thedeicoach
Check out The DEI Coach Website: www.thedeicoach.com

Erika Jefferson
President & Founder, BWISE

Erika Jefferson is the President and Founder of Black Women in Science and Engineering (BWISE), an organization focused on bridging the leadership gap for Black women in STEM. She received her MBA from Georgia Tech and her BS in Chemical Engineering from LSU. She has worked for top companies such as Amoco, BP, Chevron, and Praxair in a myriad of leadership and executive roles ranging from sales / business development to supply chain and operations excellence. Her more than two decades of experience led her across the nation from Chicago, to Greenville, Charlotte, Atlanta and eventually Houston.

ABOUT BWISE

Black Women in Science & Engineering (BWISE) was founded in 2015 with the purpose to support underrepresented women through networking, mentorship and career development. The group consists of black women from middle management through senior leadership with degrees in the sciences, math and engineering (even if they no longer work in that field) who would like to connect with others. The organization provides a platform and a space to share career experiences and be encouraged. The BWISE focus is on career advancement through personal and professional development.

Follow Erika and BWISE:
Website: www.bwiseusa.org
Twitter: https://twitter.com/bwise_bwiseusa
Facebook: https://www.facebook.com/groups/1096135527127468/
LinkedIn: https://www.linkedin.com/groups/8428298/profile
YouTube: https://www.youtube.com/channel/
UC2GWuiAJgl3s_MOVgo4KXJA

#BWISEHiddenFigures

Author Biography

D ana is an infectious soul with a cheerful outlook on all the experience life grants you! She has a heart full of love for family, friends, and community, and if that wasn't enough, she has over 30 years of life and professional experience in the corporate world. Dana diligently climbed the corporate ladder, starting as an administrative assistant all the way to Senior Vice President while balancing raising a family of 6 children (giving her 3 grandchildren thus far) with her husband Trevor and still pursuing educational elevation. Dana credits the key to this successful journey as self-confidence.

She learned to develop self-confidence during her journey, which had far-reaching implications that positively affected her relationships, health, and career, creating joy with real quality of life. Gaining and sustaining confidence profoundly affected Dana's overall quality of life. As she began to trust herself and cultivate self-assurance, she was able to stay focused, motivated, and resilient in facing challenges or setbacks. Her growing confidence encouraged her to go after opportunities that helped further her growth and development. Unbeknownst at the time, it was giving her the courage to take control of her life with things such as (most importantly) choosing to make decisions based on what aligned with her values and goals, being present, interacting without fear and hesitation, and fostering strong, healthy relationships with her family (especially her adult children) and others. Her health improved merely because she was encouraged to take better care of herself through exercise and other self-care activities such as sleep and healthy eating. Dana is adamant that self-confidence protected her against feelings of insecurity and inadequacy that could have severely restricted her potential.

Dana's love to see people grow, develop, and achieve a fulfilling and satisfying life inspired her to author this book sharing critical lessons she learned during her climb up the corporate ladder. Her mission is to provide opportunities for others with similar aspirations who have doubt that it is possible to achieve without sacrificing their health or neglecting their relationships, showing that anything is possible with a vision, diligent efforts, self-dedication, and the right team. You can create lasting personal and professional success, setting you up for an incredibly fulfilling future! So come along and enjoy the journey as you create your balanced, successful life!